Umbria Tr[avel]

Guide 2023-2024

A Journey Through Italy's Timeless
Heartland

David Carter

Welcome to Umbria

Table of Content

Chapter One

Introduction

Embark on an Unparalleled Journey Through Umbria

Welcome to the definitive travel guide to Umbria – your passport to discovering Italy's best-kept secret. If you're seeking an authentic and enriching adventure, you've found the perfect companion. This book is not just a guide; it's your key to unlocking the heart and soul of this captivating region.

What sets this travel guide apart is its commitment to uncovering the hidden treasures of Umbria. Beyond the well-trodden paths, we delve into the lesser-known corners, revealing charming villages, tranquil landscapes, and experiences that often escape the typical tourist radar. Prepare to explore Umbria like a local, embracing its untouched beauty and authentic spirit.

Crafted with meticulous attention to detail, this guide curates experiences that cater to every traveler's interests. Whether you're an art enthusiast, a nature lover, a history buff, or a culinary connoisseur, our recommendations are tailored to make your journey unforgettable. From cultural festivals to secluded hiking trails, we provide diverse activities that resonate with your passions.

What truly makes this guide the ultimate companion is the inclusion of insights from locals who call Umbria home. You'll gain access to genuine recommendations, hidden gems, and off-the-beaten-path adventures that only those intimately familiar with the region can share. This insider knowledge ensures that your trip goes beyond the surface and delves into the heart of Umbria.

Indulge in Umbria's rich culinary heritage with our carefully curated list of restaurants, markets, and traditional eateries. Taste the region's flavors through its signature dishes, accompanied by locally produced wines that add a perfect touch to your gastronomic journey. Immerse yourself in the local culture by participating in festivals, workshops, and interactions that connect you with the vibrant people of Umbria.

We comprehend that traveling may be both thrilling and intimidating. To make your journey seamless, we've provided detailed maps, transportation options, and practical tips to navigate the region with ease.

Whether you're a solo traveler, a couple on a romantic getaway, or a family seeking bonding moments, this guide ensures you make the most of your time in Umbria.

As you flip through these pages, envision the memories you'll create – the sunsets over rolling hills, the laughter shared in bustling town squares, and the awe-inspiring architecture that transports you to another era. This book isn't just about information; it's about crafting your own story in the enchanting narrative of Umbria.

So, why is this the best travel guide for your journey through Umbria?

Because it's more than a guide; it's an invitation to experience the region in its entirety. It's a companion that ensures you explore, savor, and cherish every moment, leaving you with memories that will last a lifetime.

Get ready to embark on a remarkable journey through Umbria. The adventure starts now.

History and Cultural Significance

Exploring Umbria's Rich Heritage

Umbria, a region steeped in history and cultural significance, invites you to journey through time and immerse yourself in its captivating story. From ancient civilizations to medieval wonders, Umbria's heritage resonates in its architecture, art, and way of life.

Etruscan Origins and Roman Influence

The roots of Umbria's history trace back to the Etruscan civilization, one of Italy's earliest inhabitants. Etruscan ruins, artifacts, and tombs stand as a testament to their legacy. With the rise of the Roman Empire, Umbria became an integral part of the Roman heartland, and remnants of this era can be explored in towns like Assisi and Spoleto.

Birthplace of St. Francis

Umbria's spiritual significance is highlighted by being the birthplace of one of the most renowned saints in Italy (St. Francis of Assisi). His teachings of humility, compassion, and the connection between man and nature shaped not only the region but also resonated globally. The Basilica of St. Francis in Assisi stands as a beacon of his legacy, attracting pilgrims and admirers from around the world.

Medieval Towns and Artistic Heritage

Umbria's medieval towns, characterized by narrow streets and towering fortresses, are living relics of the Middle Ages. These towns, including Perugia, Gubbio, and Orvieto, hold a rich tapestry of Gothic and Renaissance architecture, captivating visitors with their timeless charm. Renowned artists like Perugino and Giotto left their mark on the region, with their masterpieces adorning churches and museums.

Cultural Resilience and Traditions

Umbria's history is a story of resilience, as it preserved its culture and traditions despite external influences. Festivals like the Festival dei Due Mondi in Spoleto and

Calendimaggio in Assisi celebrate the region's artistic and cultural heritage. Artisan crafts, such as ceramics, textiles, and woodworking, continue to thrive, showcasing the enduring spirit of Umbria's people.

A Living Tapestry

As you explore Umbria's historic towns, walk its cobblestone streets, and immerse yourself in its local life, you'll come to appreciate how its history and culture have woven an intricate tapestry that defines the region. From religious devotion to artistic expression, from ancient roots to modern vitality, Umbria stands as a living testament to Italy's enduring legacy.

Your journey through Umbria's history and cultural significance will transport you through the ages, offering a deeper understanding of the region's identity and its contributions to the world's cultural mosaic. As you stand in awe of architectural marvels and experience time-honored traditions, you'll realize that in Umbria, history is not just a relic of the past; it's a vibrant force that shapes the present and future.

Nearby Major Cities

Exploring Umbria's Strategic Locale

Nestled in the heart of Italy, Umbria enjoys a prime location that provides easy access to some of the country's most iconic cities. While Umbria stands as a captivating destination on its own, its proximity to these major urban centers adds an extra layer of convenience and diversity to your Italian adventure.

Rome

The Eternal City

Umbria's strategic location places it just a train ride away from Rome, the legendary capital that needs no introduction. From the grandeur of the Colosseum to the artistry of the Vatican City, Rome's historical, artistic, and cultural significance is unparalleled. Marvel at ancient ruins, relish delectable cuisine and immerse yourself in a metropolis that bridges antiquity and modernity.

Florence

Renaissance Splendor

For lovers of art, architecture, and the Renaissance, Florence is a treasure trove waiting to be explored. Within a few hours journey from Umbria, you can stroll along the Arno River, gaze at Michelangelo's David, and step inside the Uffizi Gallery to witness masterpieces that shaped Western art. Florence's enchanting atmosphere resonates through its narrow streets and stunning piazzas.

Perugia

Your Gateway to Tuscany

Umbria's capital city, Perugia, serves as a gateway not only to the region but also to the neighboring beauty of Tuscany. Situated conveniently between Florence and Rome, Perugia offers a blend of urban vibrancy and medieval charm. As you explore its historic center and indulge in its renowned chocolate, you'll find yourself at the crossroads of Italy's most beloved regions.

Siena

Medieval Marvels

Venture slightly further into Tuscany, and you'll encounter Siena, a city renowned for its medieval architecture and the famous Palio horse race. The Piazza del Campo, surrounded by elegant palaces, serves as a hub of activity and a window into Siena's storied past. Revel in the city's distinct character and artistic heritage as you roam its cobbled streets.

Assisi

Spiritual and Artistic Center

Assisi's proximity to major cities like Florence and Rome enhances its appeal as a spiritual and artistic center. While Assisi itself is a haven of religious significance and historical charm, its location allows you to easily extend your journey to explore the broader cultural and artistic tapestry of Italy.

Umbria's position at the crossroads of these major cities ensures that your travel experience is enriched with diversity. Whether you're drawn to the grandeur of Rome, the cultural riches of Florence, or the medieval allure of Perugia, Umbria stands as a perfect starting point or a peaceful retreat, offering you the best of both worlds. Embrace the unique flavor of each city, and let Umbria be your link to Italy's most iconic destinations.

Chapter Two

Planning Your Trip to Umbria

Planning a trip to Umbria, Italy's picturesque heartland, is an exciting endeavor. From the best time to visit and get around the region to where to stay, understanding the weather, and preparing for local customs, here's a comprehensive guide to help you make the most of your Umbrian adventure.

When to Visit

Umbria's beauty shines year-round, but the best time to visit depends on your preferences. Spring (April to June) offers pleasant weather, blooming landscapes, and lively festivals. Summer (July to August) is warm and bustling with events, making it ideal for outdoor activities. Fall (September to October) brings milder weather, harvest festivals, and vibrant foliage. Winter (November to February) is less crowded, offering a chance to enjoy the region's cozy charm and unique Christmas traditions.

Getting Around

Umbria's efficient transportation options make exploring easy. For longer distances, consider arriving by air at Perugia Airport or nearby airports like Rome's Fiumicino Airport. Traveling by train from major cities like Rome and Florence provides scenic journeys and convenient access to towns like Perugia, Assisi, and Orvieto. Renting a car offers the flexibility to explore remote areas and charming villages at your own pace. Local buses and trains within Umbria provide efficient connections between towns.

Where to Stay

Umbria offers a range of accommodation options to suit every traveler's preference. From luxury hotels and charming boutique inns to agriturismi (farm stays) and vacation rentals, you'll find accommodations that reflect the region's character. Staying in historical town centers immerses you in local life, while countryside retreats offer relaxation amid scenic landscapes. Booking accommodations in advance is recommended, especially during peak travel seasons.

Weather and Preparation

Umbria's weather varies throughout the year, so packing accordingly is essential. Spring and fall call for layers, as temperatures can change rapidly. Summers are warm, so bring lightweight clothing, sunscreen, and a hat. Winters can be chilly, especially in higher elevations, so pack warm clothing. Umbrellas and rain gear are useful year-round due to occasional showers. Comfortable walking shoes are a must, as exploring towns often involves strolling cobblestone streets.

Timezones

Umbria operates on Central European Time (CET), which is

UTC+1. During Daylight Saving Time (DST), the region follows Central European Summer Time (CEST), which is UTC+2. Be sure to adjust your plans and reservations accordingly if traveling during the DST period (usually from the last Sunday in March to the last Sunday in October).

Language and Currency

Italian is the official language in Umbria and throughout Italy. While English is commonly spoken in tourist areas, learning a few basic Italian phrases can enhance your travel experience. The official currency is the Euro (EUR), and credit cards are widely accepted. ATMs are readily available in towns and cities for convenient cash withdrawals.

Cultural Etiquette

Umbria's culture embraces warmth and respect. Greet locals with a friendly "Buongiorno" (good morning) or "Buonasera" (good evening). When visiting churches or religious sites, dress modestly. Tipping is not as common as in some other countries, but leaving a small tip is appreciated. Engaging with locals and learning about their customs enhances your journey.

As you plan your journey to Umbria, consider your interests, the time of year, and the experiences you wish to have. By understanding the region's weather, transportation options, and local customs, you'll be well-prepared to create cherished memories in this enchanting Italian region.

Chapter Three

Getting to Umbria

Your Pathway to the Heart of Italy

Umbria's central location in Italy makes it easily accessible through various modes of transportation. Whether you're arriving from other parts of Italy or international destinations, getting to Umbria is a seamless journey that sets the stage for your unforgettable adventure.

By Air

Arriving at Nearby Airports

Umbria is conveniently connected to several nearby airports, making air travel a popular choice for visitors. The closest major airport is Perugia San Francesco d'Assisi - Umbria International Airport. This modern airport serves both domestic and limited international flights, offering a convenient entry point for travelers seeking direct access to the region. Another option is **Leonardo da Vinci - Fiumicino Airport** in Rome, which is well-connected to various international destinations. From these airports, you can easily reach Umbria by renting a car, taking a train, or using shuttle services.

By Train

Efficient Rail Connections

Italy's efficient and extensive rail network offers excellent connections to Umbria. The major cities of Rome and Florence serve as key rail hubs, providing direct train services to various towns within Umbria. High-speed trains like the Frecciarossa and regional trains ensure that you can reach destinations like Perugia, Assisi, and Orvieto with ease. For example, you can take a high-speed train from Rome's Termini Station to Perugia in about 1.5 hours, enjoying scenic views along the way.

By Car

Scenic Road Trips

Embark on a scenic road trip to Umbria and savor the picturesque landscapes along the way. The region is well-connected by highways, and driving offers the flexibility to explore charming villages and hidden corners at your own pace. Major roadways like the A1 and the E45 connect Umbria to other parts of Italy, allowing for a road adventure filled with breathtaking vistas. For instance, you can drive from Florence to Assisi, enjoying the stunning Tuscan and Umbrian countryside.

By Bus

Comfortable Long-Distance Travel

Long-distance buses connect major Italian cities to various towns in Umbria. This option is both economical and comfortable, providing an alternative for travelers who prefer a more relaxed and budget-friendly journey. Bus services from major cities like Rome and Florence are well-established, making it accessible to explore the region by bus. For instance, you can take a long-distance bus from Rome's

Tiburtina Station to Perugia, enjoying a hassle-free ride.

Local Transportation

Navigating Umbria

Once you've arrived in Umbria, navigating the region is made easy with an efficient local transportation system. Buses and trains provide connectivity between towns, allowing you to explore multiple destinations without hassle. Car rentals and taxis are also available, offering convenience for personalized travel within Umbria's picturesque landscapes. For instance, you can use local buses to travel from Perugia to

Assisi or take a regional train to explore other charming towns.

Umbria's strategic location ensures that getting to this enchanting region is a straightforward and enjoyable experience. Whether you choose the convenience of air travel, the charm of a road trip, or the comfort of rail connections, your journey to Umbria is a prelude to the remarkable experiences that await. As you embark on this pathway to the heart of Italy, let the anticipation of exploring Umbria's cultural treasures and natural beauty fill your travel spirit.

Chapter Four

Exploring Umbria's Top Destinations

Unveiling the Charms of the Region

Nestled within the heart of Italy lies Umbria, a captivating region brimming with history, culture, and breathtaking landscapes. As you embark on your journey through this enchanting part of the country, prepare to discover a collection of top destinations that each holds its unique allure. From medieval towns and spiritual havens to artistic centers and architectural wonders, Umbria's top destinations promise a remarkable tapestry of experiences that will leave an indelible mark on your travel memories. Join us as we uncover the gems that await in each corner of this timeless region.

Perugia

Where History and Modernity Converge

Perugia, the capital city of Umbria, is a captivating blend of history, culture, and vibrant modern life. Perched atop a hill with commanding views of the surrounding countryside, this medieval city offers a rich tapestry of experiences for visitors.

Historical Marvels

Perugia's historic center is a maze of narrow streets, medieval buildings, and well-preserved Etruscan walls. The Piazza IV Novembre serves as the heart of the city, home to the stunning Fontana Maggiore and the awe-inspiring Palazzo dei Priori – one of Italy's best-preserved medieval municipal buildings.

Art and Learning

Home to the renowned University of Perugia, the city boasts a youthful energy that complements its historical charm. The National

Gallery of Umbria showcases a rich collection of artwork from the region, spanning various periods and styles.

Chocolate and Gastronomy

A trip to the Perugina Chocolate Factory provides a tasty look into the craft of chocolate-making. Perugia is known for its delicious chocolates. Explore local markets and trattorias to savor Umbria's culinary delights, including savory truffle dishes and hearty pasta.

Festivals and Events

Perugia hosts a variety of events throughout the year, including the world-renowned Umbria Jazz Festival, attracting music enthusiasts from around the globe. The annual Eurochocolate Festival celebrates all things chocolate and is a true treat for the senses.

Panoramic Views

Climb to the Rocca Paolina, a fortress turned into an underground city, to enjoy panoramic vistas of Perugia's rooftops and the Umbrian landscape beyond. The city's elevated location provides breathtaking views that inspire awe at any time of day.

Student Spirit and Local Life

Perugia's large student population infuses the city with a dynamic atmosphere. Cafés, bookshops, and lively squares create a welcoming environment for both locals and visitors, inviting you to experience the rhythm of daily life.

Perugia's harmonious blend of history, culture, and contemporary vitality invites you to wander its charming streets, embrace its artistic soul, and immerse yourself in the warmth of its local communities. As you explore the city's treasures, you'll uncover the layers of its past while creating memories that will remain with you long after your visit.

Assisi

A Spiritual Haven and Artistic Gem

Nestled on the slopes of Mount Subasio, Assisi is a town of profound spirituality, rich history, and stunning beauty. This UNESCO World Heritage site is renowned for its connection to St. Francis, making it a spiritual pilgrimage destination for many. Beyond its religious significance, Assisi offers a tapestry of art, architecture, and breathtaking landscapes.

Basilica of St. Francis

The Basilica of San Francesco d'Assisi is a masterpiece of Italian Gothic architecture and a testament to the life and teachings of St. Francis. Its awe-inspiring frescoes by artists like Giotto and Cimabue depict scenes from the life of St. Francis and are among the most significant art collections in Italy.

Basilica of St. Clare

Dedicated to St. Clare, a follower of St. Francis, the Basilica of Santa Chiara is another architectural marvel. Its elegant facade and serene interior hold the remains of St. Clare and offer a space for reflection and reverence.

Charming Streets and Squares

Assisi's enchanting streets wind through the town, revealing charming squares, artisan shops, and picturesque alleys. The Piazza del Comune is a central gathering place, bordered by historic buildings and lively cafés that invite you to soak in the local atmosphere.

Stunning Views

For panoramic views of Assisi and the surrounding countryside, climb to the Rocca Maggiore, a medieval fortress overlooking the town. The elevated vantage point offers a breathtaking perspective that St. Francis himself would have admired.

Spiritual Experience

Assisi's spiritual aura is palpable, and pilgrims and visitors find solace in its tranquil settings. Follow in the footsteps of St. Francis by visiting the Hermitage of the Carceri, a collection of peaceful caves in the woods where he sought refuge and solitude.

Cultural Festivals

Assisi celebrates its heritage through various cultural events. The Calendimaggio Festival in May brings the medieval past to life with historical reenactments, parades, and pageantry. The town's streets become a stage, transporting you back in time.

Art and Inspiration

Assisi's artistic legacy extends beyond religious sites. Galleries and workshops showcase local craftsmanship, from ceramics to traditional textiles, offering a chance to take a piece of Assisi's creativity home with you.

Assisi is a place where spirituality, art, and nature converge to create an enriching and contemplative experience. Whether you're seeking a connection to St. Francis's teachings, artistic inspiration, or simply a serene escape, Assisi's captivating charm will leave an indelible mark on your heart and soul.

Gubbio

Where Timeless Beauty Meets Historic Grandeur

Nestled in the foothills of the Apennine Mountains, Gubbio is a medieval gem that captivates with its picturesque setting, ancient architecture, and a sense of timelessness. As you wander its cobblestone streets and gaze at its impressive landmarks, you'll feel like you've stepped back in time to a world of grandeur and charm.

Palazzo dei Consoli

Gubbio's most iconic landmark, the Palazzo dei Consoli, stands as a testament to the town's historical significance. This medieval palace overlooks the main square and houses the Eugenio Ciani Art Museum, where you can explore an impressive collection of paintings, sculptures, and archaeological artifacts.

Roman Theater

Step into history at the Roman Theater, one of the best-preserved Roman theaters in Italy. Carved into the hillside, this ancient structure once hosted theatrical performances and is a fascinating glimpse into Gubbio's Roman past.

Corsa dei Ceri Festival

Gubbio's annual Corsa dei Ceri festival is a spectacular event that showcases the town's strong sense of community and tradition. Held on May 15th, locals carry enormous wooden statues (ceri) through the streets, honoring the town's patron saints in a spirited and vibrant procession.

Majestic Views

For breathtaking panoramic views of Gubbio and its surrounding landscapes, take a cable car ride up to Monte Ingino. At the summit, you'll find the Basilica of St. Ubaldo, which houses the remains of the town's patron saint.

Medieval Charm

As you stroll through Gubbio's medieval streets, you'll encounter charming shops, artisan workshops, and inviting cafes. The town's intimate atmosphere invites you to slow down and savor its timeless beauty.

Festival of the Middle Ages

Experience Gubbio's medieval past come to life during the Festival of the Middle Ages, held in August. The town transforms into a medieval village, with parades, jousting tournaments, and traditional performances that transport you back in time.

Historic Elegance

Gubbio's architecture tells a story of its past, with medieval towers, churches, and palaces adorning the landscape. The town's well-preserved heritage creates an ambiance of historic elegance around every corner.

Gubbio's blend of history, culture, and natural beauty makes it a destination that lingers in your memory. Whether you're drawn to its ancient monuments, its lively festivals, or simply its enchanting ambiance, Gubbio offers a journey through time that's both captivating and unforgettable.

Orvieto

A Renaissance Jewel Perched in the Clouds

Perched high on a volcanic plateau, Orvieto is a captivating town that combines breathtaking scenery with a rich artistic heritage. From its stunning cathedral to its labyrinthine underground passages, Orvieto offers a blend of history, culture, and architectural wonders that leave an indelible mark on every traveler.

Orvieto Cathedral

The Orvieto Cathedral, also known as the Duomo di Orvieto, is a masterpiece of Italian Gothic architecture. Its intricate façade, adorned with intricate mosaics and sculptures, is a testament to the town's historical and artistic importance.

St. Patrick's Well

Descend into the depths of the earth to explore the ingenious St. Patrick's Well. This remarkable feat of engineering was designed to provide water during times of siege and drought. Its double-helix staircase allows visitors to descend without crossing paths with those ascending, creating a seamless flow of movement.

Orvieto Underground

Explore the mysterious labyrinth of tunnels and chambers beneath Orvieto through the Orvieto Underground. This subterranean world unveils the town's history, from ancient Etruscan origins to medieval storage facilities.

Palazzo del Popolo

Orvieto's Palazzo del Popolo is a beautiful example of medieval civic architecture. Its elegant façade and grand interior serve as a backdrop for cultural events and exhibitions.

Pozzo della Cava

Delve further into Orvieto's underground history at the Pozzo della Cava, a series of Etruscan caves and tunnels. This archaeological site provides insights into ancient life and reveals the layers of history that have shaped the town.

Etruscan Heritage

Orvieto's connection to its Etruscan past is evident in its archaeological sites, including the Necropolis of Crocifisso del Tufo. These remnants offer a glimpse into the region's pre-Roman history.

Art and Craftsmanship

Orvieto's artistic legacy is evident in its galleries, workshops, and craft stores. The town's artistic spirit is embodied in its ceramics, textiles, and traditional crafts that make for unique souvenirs.

Panoramic Vistas

Orvieto's elevated position offers stunning panoramic views of the surrounding Umbrian countryside. Climb the Torre del Moro for a breathtaking perspective that showcases the beauty of the region.

Orvieto's blend of architectural marvels, subterranean mysteries, and artistic treasures invites you to explore its depths and heights. Whether you're drawn to its spiritual landmarks, its historical intrigue, or simply its scenic vistas, Orvieto promises a journey of discovery that harmoniously weaves the past and the present.

Spoleto

A Harmonious Blend of History and Culture

Nestled in the Umbrian hills, Spoleto is a town that exudes elegance and charm, showcasing its rich history through its architecture, cultural events, and stunning natural surroundings. With its ancient ruins, medieval structures, and vibrant arts scene, Spoleto invites you to immerse yourself in its captivating ambiance.

Rocca Albornoziana

The imposing Rocca Albornoziana is a fortress that stands as a symbol of Spoleto's historical significance. This medieval castle offers panoramic views of the town and surrounding landscape, providing a glimpse into the region's past.

Cathedral of Santa Maria Assunta

The Cathedral of Santa Maria Assunta is a masterpiece of Romanesque architecture. Its intricate façade and interior are adorned with stunning frescoes and intricate details that tell the story of Spoleto's artistic heritage.

Ponti delle Torri

The Ponti delle Torri, a pair of medieval bridges with towering arches, is an iconic Spoleto landmark. Spanning a picturesque gorge, these bridges offer a stunning backdrop for exploration and photography.

Festival dei Due Mondi

Spoleto's Festival dei Due Mondi (Festival of the Two Worlds) is a renowned international arts festival that celebrates music, theater, dance, and visual arts. Held annually, this event transforms the town into a vibrant cultural hub, attracting artists and visitors from around the world.

San Pietro Church

The Church of San Pietro is a hidden gem that boasts intricate mosaics and beautiful architecture. Its quiet atmosphere and stunning artwork make it a serene place for reflection.

Historic Center

Wandering through Spoleto's historic center is a journey through time. Cobblestone streets, charming squares, and medieval buildings create an enchanting ambiance that invites exploration.

Roman Theater

The well-preserved Roman Theater is a testament to Spoleto's ancient roots. It once hosted theatrical performances and serves as a reminder of the town's historical importance.

Natural Beauty

Surrounded by rolling hills and lush greenery, Spoleto is an ideal base for outdoor enthusiasts. Hiking trails, bike routes, and scenic landscapes offer opportunities to connect with nature.

Spoleto's fusion of ancient heritage and contemporary culture creates a harmonious blend that's both captivating and inviting. Whether you're drawn to its historical landmarks, its vibrant arts scene, or its scenic landscapes, Spoleto promises an enriching journey that unfolds amid its timeless charm.

Chapter Five

Umbria's Nature and Countryside

A Serene Retreat

Beyond its charming towns and cultural treasures, Umbria's natural landscapes and picturesque countryside beckon travelers seeking tranquility and beauty. From rolling hills and vineyards to serene lakes and lush forests, the region's connection to nature offers a peaceful escape and a chance to reconnect with the earth.

7 days Road Trip

Exploring the Picturesque Landscape of Umbria

Embarking on a road trip through Umbria's stunning landscape is a journey of awe-inspiring views, charming villages, and serene countryside. This itinerary will take you through some of the region's most captivating destinations, allowing you to immerse yourself in its natural beauty and rich culture.

Day 1

Arrival in Perugia

Arrive in Perugia, the capital of Umbria, and explore its historic center.

Wander through Piazza IV Novembre, visit the Fontana Maggiore, and admire the Palazzo dei Priori.

Enjoy dinner at a local trattoria and savor Umbrian cuisine.

Day 2

Assisi and Spiritual Serenity

Drive to Assisi, known for its spiritual significance and artistic heritage.

Visit the Basilica of San Francesco d'Assisi, adorned with mesmerizing frescoes.

Explore the Basilica of Santa Chiara and stroll through the town's peaceful streets.

Take in panoramic views from the Rocca Maggiore.

Day 3

Charming Gubbio and Medieval Marvels

Depart for Gubbio, a medieval gem nestled in the hills.

Explore the Palazzo dei Consoli and immerse yourself in the town's history.

Visit the Basilica of Sant'Ubaldo and experience the Corsa dei Ceri festival (if timing allows).

Enjoy dinner at a local osteria, savoring regional flavors.

Day 4

Orvieto's Heights and Hidden Delights

Drive to Orvieto, perched atop a volcanic plateau.

Marvel at the grandeur of the Orvieto Cathedral and its intricate façade.

Descend into the St. Patrick's Well and explore the underground passages.

Wander through Orvieto's charming streets and enjoy the ambiance.

Day 5

Lake Trasimeno's Tranquility

Head to Lake Trasimeno and relax by its shores.

Consider a boat ride to explore the lake's islands or a leisurely hike along its trails.

Enjoy a lakeside picnic or dine at a waterfront restaurant.

Day 6

Vineyards and Countryside Retreat

Venture along the Sagrantino Wine Route, passing through vineyards and olive groves.

Enjoy wine tastings at local wineries and savor the flavors of Umbrian wines.

Consider staying in a countryside agriturismo for an authentic experience.

Day 7

Scenic Drive and Farewell

Embark on a leisurely drive through Umbria's rolling hills and picturesque landscapes.

Stop at charming villages along the way, capturing the essence of rural life.

Return to Perugia or continue your journey to other destinations in Italy.

Tips

Plan your road trip according to the time of year, as each season offers a different charm.

Think about making reservations in advance, especially during the busiest travel seasons.

Embrace the local cuisine and indulge in regional dishes and wines.

Take your time to savor each destination and explore off-the-beaten-path spots.

Capture the breathtaking landscapes with your camera to relive the memories.

Embarking on a road trip through Umbria's landscape is a chance to immerse yourself in the region's natural beauty, historical richness, and warm culture. As you traverse its scenic roads and embrace the charm of its towns, you'll create a tapestry of unforgettable experiences that showcase the best of this enchanting Italian region.

Chapter Six

Hiking, Biking, and Outdoor Activities in Umbria

Umbria's diverse landscape provide the perfect playground for outdoor enthusiasts seeking hiking trails, biking routes, and other exciting activities. From the hills and forests to the lakeshores and charming villages, the region offers a wealth of opportunities to connect with nature and embrace the thrill of adventure.

Hiking Trails

Monte Subasio: Hike to the summit of Monte Subasio near Assisi for panoramic views and a chance to explore the Hermitage of the Carceri, a series of peaceful caves in the woods.

Monte Cucco: Discover the beauty of the Monte Cucco Regional Park, where hiking trails lead to stunning viewpoints, caves, and lush meadows.

La Valle del Menotre: Follow this picturesque trail that winds through the Menotre Valley, passing by charming villages and offering glimpses of the region's rural beauty.

Biking Routes

Umbria Bike Itinerary: Explore Umbria's landscapes on two wheels with the Umbria Bike Itinerary, a network of cycling paths that traverse the region's diverse terrains.

Lake Trasimeno Cycling: Circumnavigate Lake Trasimeno by bike, enjoying lakeside views and passing through charming towns along the way.

Vineyard Routes: Embark on a biking adventure along the Sagrantino Wine Route, pedaling through vineyards and olive groves while savoring the region's culinary delights.

Water Activities

Lake Trasimeno: Rent a kayak or paddleboard to explore the calm waters of Lake Trasimeno, or take a boat ride to visit the islands and enjoy the serene ambiance.

Rafting and Kayaking: Experience the thrill of white-water rafting or kayaking in the Nera River, an exciting way to discover Umbria's natural beauty.

Climbing and Adventure Parks

Umbria Climbing Areas: For rock climbing enthusiasts, Umbria offers several climbing areas, such as

Ferentillo and Castel Giorgio, where you can challenge your skills and enjoy scenic views.

Adventure Parks: If you're traveling with family, consider visiting adventure parks like the "Parco Avventura Nahar" near Lake Trasimeno, offering zip lines, ropes courses, and more.

Hot Air Balloon Rides

Soar above Umbria's landscapes in a hot air balloon for a unique perspective of the region's hills, towns, and natural beauty.

Horseback Riding

Explore Umbria's countryside on horseback, following trails that lead through vineyards, olive groves, and picturesque villages.

Tips

Plan your outdoor activities based on your interests and skill level.

Check weather conditions and prepare accordingly, especially for longer hikes or biking routes.

Rent equipment if needed, or bring your gear for specific activities.

Respect the environment by following Leave No Trace principles and local regulations.

Embrace the local culture and cuisine, as many outdoor activities can be complemented by culinary experiences.

Umbria's outdoor playground invites adventurers of all levels to explore its natural wonders, from the heights of its hills to the shores of its lakes. Whether you're seeking adrenaline-pumping thrills or serene nature walks, the region's diverse offerings ensure that every outdoor enthusiast can find their perfect adventure.

Chapter Seven

Shopping in Umbria

Unveiling Unique Treasures and Local Finds

Umbria's vibrant shopping scene offers an array of treasures, from artisanal crafts and gourmet delights to high-end fashion and antiques. Here are some specific examples of what you can discover while shopping in this enchanting Italian region:

Local Artisanal Crafts

Ceramics from Deruta: Explore the charming town of Deruta and discover hand-painted ceramics, such as intricately designed plates, bowls, and tiles.

Textiles in Perugia: Visit boutique shops in Perugia for luxurious handwoven textiles, including linens, fabrics, and exquisite tapestries.

Leather Goods in Assisi: Explore boutiques in Assisi offering finely crafted leather products, from stylish bags and belts to wallets and accessories.

Food and Culinary Delights

Truffle Products: Indulge in the earthy aroma of Umbrian truffles by purchasing truffle oil, truffle-infused sauces, and even whole truffles.

Umbrian Olive Oil: Take home bottles of locally produced extra virgin olive oil, known for its rich flavor and distinct quality.

Umbrian Wines: Select bottles of renowned Umbrian wines, such as the bold Sagrantino or the crisp Orvieto, to enjoy a taste of the region's vineyards.

Local Markets

Perugia's Mercato Coperto: Immerse yourself in the bustling atmosphere of Perugia's covered market, where you can find fresh produce, cheeses, meats, and local specialties.

Assisi's Piazza del Comune: Experience the weekly market in Assisi's central square, offering everything from clothing to local food products.

Fashion and Boutiques

Designer Labels in Perugia: Explore Perugia's boutique-lined streets for Italian fashion brands and designer labels, offering clothing, accessories, and shoes.

Antique Shops

Gubbio's Antique Stores: Wander through Gubbio's antique shops to discover vintage furniture, intricate decorations, and collectibles that carry the echoes of the past.

Art Galleries and Workshops:

Art Galleries in Assisi: Peruse galleries showcasing local artists' paintings, sculptures, and unique artistic creations that capture the spirit of the region.

Ceramic Workshops: Join workshops in Deruta to witness the intricate process of creating the town's renowned hand-painted ceramics.

Specialty Shops

Perugina Chocolate: Delight in Perugina's famous Baci chocolates, available in various flavors and packaging, making for delightful souvenirs.

Herbal Shops in Spello: Discover Spello's herbal shops, offering aromatic teas, natural cosmetics, and herbal remedies made from locally sourced ingredients.

Weekly Markets

Todi Market: Explore Todi's market for a selection of local products, crafts, clothing, and household items, creating a colorful bazaar of treasures.

Umbria's shopping experiences are as diverse as the region itself, offering a blend of history, artistry, and flavors that reflect its unique identity. As you explore its markets, boutiques, and workshops, you'll have the opportunity to immerse yourself in the local culture and bring home a piece of Umbria's distinctive charm.

Chapter Eight

Food and Drinks in Umbria

A Gastronomic Journey Through Taste and Tradition

Umbria's culinary scene is a symphony of flavors, blending age-old recipes with locally sourced ingredients to create dishes that evoke the region's history and culture. From quaint trattorias to fine dining establishments, your taste buds are in for a treat as you explore the following delectable offerings:

Truffle Treasures

Tagliatelle al Tartufo Nero: Relish in the earthy elegance of black truffles atop fresh Tagliatelle pasta at restaurants across the region.

Bianchetto Truffle Risotto: Savor the delicate aroma of bianchetto truffles infused into creamy risotto, a must-try delight.

Sip Umbrian Olive Oil

Agriturismo Experiences: Book a stay at an agriturismo like Le Silve di Armenzano near Assisi, where you can taste olive oil produced on-site.

Local Markets: Sample freshly pressed olive oil at Perugia's Mercato

Coperto and chat with producers about their craftsmanship.

Heartwarming Staples

Strangozzi all'Umbra: Enjoy the distinct flavors of strangozzi pasta served with traditional Umbrian tomato sauce, garlic, and black olives.

Porchetta Sandwiches: Satisfy your cravings with a porchetta sandwich from food stalls in towns like Norcia and Spello.

Cheese and Charcuterie

Cured Meat Delights: Delve into the world of wild boar salami and prosciutto di Norcia at local butcher shops and markets.

Pecorino di Norcia: Sample the rich, tangy flavors of Pecorino di Norcia, perfectly complemented by local honey.

Traditional Stews and Game

Cinghiale Stew: Dive into the flavors of the Umbrian game with pappardelle al cinghiale, a pasta dish featuring wild boar sauce.

Umbrian Lentil Stew: Savor the hearty Umbrian lentil stew, a nourishing dish often enjoyed during colder months.

Sagrantino Wines

Wine Routes: Embark on the Strada del Sagrantino, exploring vineyards and cellars to sample the robust Sagrantino di Montefalco.

Cantina Goretti: Visit Cantina Goretti in Perugia for guided wine tours and tastings of their acclaimed Sagrantino wines.

Dolci Delights

Torta al Testo: Treat yourself to torta al testo, a flatbread often filled with prosciutto, cheese, and vegetables, offering a delightful contrast of textures.

Umbrian Sweets: Indulge in torcolo, a traditional ring-shaped cake filled with nuts, dried fruits, and aromatic spices.

Food Festivals and Markets

Perugia's Eurochocolate: If visiting in October, join the chocolate festivities at Eurochocolate, a celebration of all things cocoa.

Gubbio's Sagra del Cinghiale: Immerse yourself in the Wild Boar Festival in Gubbio, celebrating the region's gastronomic heritage.

Cafè Culture and Digestivi

Caffè Italiano: Conclude your meals with an authentic Italian espresso, reveling in its strong, aromatic notes.

After-Dinner Delights: Sample local digestivi like Amaro dell'Umbria or Nocino, a walnut liqueur, for a perfect finish to your culinary adventure.

Umbria's culinary offerings are a testament to the region's dedication to preserving its heritage through food. As you explore its diverse dishes and drinks, you'll not only satisfy

your palate but also gain insight into
the soul of Umbria itself.

Chapter Nine

Entertainment and Nightlife in Umbria

A Blend of Culture and Evening Excitement

Umbria's entertainment and nightlife scene offers a harmonious blend of cultural experiences, lively events, and cozy establishments that come to life as the sun sets. From music festivals and art exhibitions to charming bars and evening strolls, there's something for everyone to enjoy after dark in this enchanting region.

Cultural Performances

Umbria Jazz Festival: Experience world-class jazz performances in Perugia during the Umbria Jazz Festival, an annual event that draws music enthusiasts from around the globe.

Folklore and Theater: Attend traditional folk performances and theater productions that showcase Umbria's cultural heritage and artistic talent.

Evening Strolls

Historic Towns at Twilight:
Wander through the charming streets
of Assisi, Gubbio, or Orvieto as the
sun sets, taking in the illuminated
facades and enchanting ambiance.

Perugia's Underground: Join
guided tours of Perugia's
underground city, a captivating
experience that unveils the city's
hidden history after dark.

Live Music Venues

Music Bars in Perugia: Discover
intimate music bars like Caffè
Morlacchi and Blu Notte, offering live

performances ranging from jazz to acoustic sets.

Clubs and Lounges: Dance the night away at Perugia's clubs like Urban and L'Altro Mondo Studios, where DJs keep the energy high.

Cinema and Theatres

Cinephile's Paradise: Catch international and independent films at Perugia's cinemas like Cinema Zenith and Cinema Cavour.

Teatro Morlacchi: Attend theater productions and cultural events at Perugia's historic Teatro Morlacchi, a venue with a rich artistic legacy.

Festive Events

Perugia's Chocolate Festival: Join the sweet celebrations of Eurochocolate, where Perugia transforms into a chocolate paradise, featuring tastings and entertainment.

Medieval Festivals: Experience medieval reenactments and festivities, such as Gubbio's Festa dei Ceri, a vibrant event celebrating the town's patron saint.

Wine and Gastronomic Experiences

Wine Tastings: Enjoy evening wine tastings at local wineries, often accompanied by regional cheeses, offering a delightful combination of flavors.

Culinary Tours: Embark on gastronomic tours that include evening visits to local trattorias and osterias, allowing you to savor Umbria's flavors.

Nighttime Views

Assisi at Night: Witness Assisi's illuminated beauty from the Rocca Maggiore or Piazza del Comune, offering panoramic views of the town under a starlit sky.

Perugia from Above: Ascend to Perugia's historic center at night for breathtaking views of the city lights twinkling below.

Cafés and Wine Bars

Piazza IV Novembre: Sip coffee or wine at cafés around Perugia's central square, Piazza IV Novembre, and enjoy the lively atmosphere.

Wine Bars in Assisi: Unwind at wine bars like Enoteca Properzio in Assisi, offering a curated selection of local wines and a cozy ambiance.

Umbria's entertainment and nightlife scene invites you to immerse yourself in its cultural richness and vibrant spirit after sunset. Whether you're seeking musical performances, artistic experiences, or simply a relaxing evening in a charming setting, Umbria offers a diverse array of options to ensure your nights are as memorable as your days.

Chapter Ten

Celebrating Local Culture

Vibrant Festivals and Traditions of Umbria

Umbria's rich history and cultural heritage are brought to life through a tapestry of festivals, traditions, and events that reflect the region's deep connection to its roots. Immerse yourself in the rhythms of life in Umbria as you participate in these vibrant celebrations:

Corsa dei Ceri in Gubbio

Date: May 15

Description: Join the exhilarating Corsa dei Ceri festival in Gubbio, a centuries-old tradition where teams race through the town carrying massive wooden statues of saints on their shoulders.

Umbria Jazz Festival in Perugia

Date: July

Description: Immerse yourself in the world of jazz during the Umbria Jazz Festival in Perugia. The city comes alive with performances by renowned artists from around the globe.

Festa dei Ceri in Gubbio

Date: May 15

Description: Experience the Festa dei Ceri, a passionate celebration of Gubbio's patron saint, Sant'Ubaldo. The town is filled with colorful processions and a vibrant atmosphere.

Calendimaggio in Assisi

Date: First week of May

Description: Transport yourself to medieval times during Calendimaggio in Assisi. This festival celebrates spring with historical reenactments, processions, music, and competitions.

Festival dei Due Mondi in Spoleto

Date: June-July

Description: Immerse yourself in the arts during the Festival dei Due Mondi in Spoleto. This internationally renowned event showcases music, theater, dance, and visual arts in various venues.

Infiorate Flower Festivals

Date: Corpus Christi (varies, usually in June)

Description: Witness the stunning Infiorate festivals in towns like Spello and Panicale, where intricate flower carpets are created on the streets to honor the religious holiday.

Palio della Balestra in Gubbio

Date: Last Sunday of May and August 14

Description: Step back in time during the Palio della Balestra, an archery competition in Gubbio that revives medieval traditions and fierce competition.

Sagra del Tulipano in Castiglione del Lago

Date: April-May

Description: Celebrate spring at the Sagra del Tulipano in Castiglione del

Lago, where colorful tulip displays, markets, and cultural events take center stage.

Processione dei Misteri in Terni

Date: Easter Sunday

Description: Experience the deeply spiritual Processione dei Misteri in Terni, a solemn and symbolic procession reenacting the events of Easter.

Umbrian Harvest Festivals

Date: Various times during the harvest season

Description: Join local communities in celebrating the bountiful harvest with fairs, feasts, and activities that honor Umbria's agricultural traditions.

Participating in these festivals and traditions offers an immersive glimpse into the heart of Umbria's culture and history. From the pulse of lively music to the solemnity of ancient rituals, these celebrations unite the past and present colorfully and memorably.

Chapter Eleven

7-day itinerary in Umbria

Unveiling the Charms of Central Italy

Day 1

Arrival in Perugia

Arrive in Perugia, the capital of Umbria.

Explore the historic center, visit Piazza IV Novembre, and admire the Fontana Maggiore.

Enjoy a traditional Umbrian dinner at a local trattoria.

Day 2

Assisi and Spiritual Exploration

Drive to St. Francis' birthplace, Assisi.

Visit the Basilica of San Francesco d'Assisi, adorned with stunning frescoes.

Explore the Basilica of Santa Chiara and the town's charming streets.

Take in panoramic views from the Rocca Maggiore.

Day 3

Gubbio's Medieval Marvels

Depart for Gubbio, a picturesque medieval town.

Explore the Palazzo dei Consoli and discover the town's history.

Visit the Basilica of Sant'Ubaldo and immerse yourself in the Corsa dei Ceri festival (if timing allows).

Day 4

Orvieto's Elegance and History

Drive to Orvieto, perched on a volcanic plateau.

Visit the Orvieto Cathedral with its intricate façade and stunning interiors.

Explore the St. Patrick's Well and stroll through the town's charming streets.

Day 5

Lake Trasimeno and Relaxation

Head to Lake Trasimeno and enjoy a leisurely day by the shores.

Consider a boat ride to explore the islands or a hike along the lakeside trails.

Indulge in a lakeside picnic or dine at a waterfront restaurant.

Day 6

Wine Route and Countryside Retreat

Venture along the Sagrantino Wine Route, passing through vineyards and olive groves.

Enjoy wine tastings at local wineries and savor Umbrian wines.

Consider staying in a countryside agriturismo for an authentic experience.

Day 7

Exploring Perugia and Departure

Spend the morning exploring more of Perugia's attractions, such as the Arco Etrusco and the Perugina Chocolate Factory.

Enjoy a final Italian meal before departing or continuing your journey to other destinations.

Tips

This itinerary offers a balance between cultural exploration, historical sites, and relaxation.

Consider visiting during spring or fall for pleasant weather and fewer crowds.

Plan your activities based on opening hours and local events.

Book accommodations in advance, especially during peak travel seasons.

Embrace local cuisine and try regional dishes in different towns.

Capture beautiful landscapes and memorable moments with your camera.

This 7-day journey through Umbria offers a glimpse into the region's history, culture, and natural beauty, leaving you with cherished memories of authentic Italian experiences.

Weekend plans in Umbria

Weekend Getaway Plans in Enchanting Umbria

Day 1

Exploring Perugia

Morning: Arrive in Perugia and settle into your accommodation.

Late Morning: Stroll through Perugia's historic center, visiting Piazza IV Novembre and the impressive Fontana Maggiore.

Afternoon: Discover the Perugina Chocolate Factory or explore the

National Archaeological Museum of Umbria.

Evening: Enjoy a traditional Umbrian dinner at a local trattoria.

Day 2

Assisi's Spiritual Charm

Morning: Depart for Assisi, the spiritual heart of Umbria.

Late Morning: Visit the stunning Basilica of San Francesco d'Assisi, home to exquisite frescoes.

Afternoon: Explore the Basilica of Santa Chiara and admire the town's panoramic views.

Evening: Savor an intimate dinner in Assisi's quaint streets.

Day 3

Gubbio's Timeless Beauty

Morning: Drive to Gubbio, a charming medieval town.

Late Morning: Explore the Palazzo dei Consoli and its intriguing history.

Afternoon: Visit the Basilica of Sant'Ubaldo and experience the town's authentic atmosphere.

Evening: Enjoy a memorable farewell dinner in Gubbio.

Tips

Prioritize sites that resonate with your interests and pace.

Check opening hours and consider making reservations for popular attractions.

Immerse yourself in the local culture by engaging with locals and trying regional cuisine.

Capture picturesque landscapes and architectural wonders with your camera.

Consider attending any local festivals or events taking place during your visit.

Plan your itinerary with relaxation in mind, leaving room for unexpected discoveries.

This weekend escape to Umbria promises an enchanting blend of history, spirituality, and authentic Italian experiences that will leave you refreshed and inspired.

Chapter Twelve

Practical Information for Your Umbria Adventure

Accommodation Options

Hotels: From boutique to luxury, Umbria offers a range of hotels in its towns and cities. Examples include Hotel Brufani Palace in Perugia and Hotel Giotto Assisi.

Agriturismi: Experience rural life by staying at agriturismi (farm stays) like Agriturismo Le Silve di Armenzano near Assisi.

Bed and Breakfasts: Enjoy personalized hospitality at B&Bs like Il Roseto in Gubbio.

Transportation Options

Car Rental: Rent a car for flexibility in exploring Umbria's countryside and reaching off-the-beaten-path destinations.

Train: The region is well-connected by trains. Traveling between cities like Perugia, Assisi, and Orvieto is convenient.

Bus: Local buses and regional lines connect towns and villages. However, schedules can be limited.

Taxi and Rideshares: Taxis and rideshare apps are available in larger towns and cities.

Currency and Tipping

Currency: The currency is the Euro (EUR).

Tipping: Tipping is not obligatory but is appreciated. Leave a small tip (usually around 5-10% of the bill) at restaurants and cafes if the service was exceptional.

Safety Tips

Personal Belongings: Keep your belongings secure, especially in crowded areas and tourist sites.

Health Precautions: Stay hydrated, use sunscreen, and wear appropriate clothing to protect against the sun. Carry a water bottle and map with you.

Emergency Numbers: The emergency number in Italy is 112 for police, medical assistance, and fire.

Health Emergency

Healthcare: Umbria has quality healthcare facilities. The main hospital in Perugia is Ospedale Santa Maria della Misericordia.

Travel Insurance: Consider travel insurance to cover potential medical expenses and emergencies.

Pharmacies: Look for the green cross sign to locate pharmacies for over-the-counter medications.

Examples of Health Emergency Scenarios

If you encounter a medical emergency, call 112 for immediate assistance. Paramedics will arrive to assess the situation.

If you need medication, visit a local pharmacy. For prescription medicines, you may need to consult a doctor or go to the emergency room.

If you experience severe symptoms like difficulty breathing or chest pain, seek medical attention promptly.

Umbria welcomes you with its warmth and charm, and with these practical insights, you'll be well-prepared to make the most of your journey while ensuring your safety and comfort throughout your stay.

Conclusion

As you draw the final curtain on your exploration of Umbria, a chapter of enchantment and discovery comes to a close, leaving you with a tapestry of memories that capture the essence of this captivating Italian region. Throughout this travel guide, we've unveiled the diverse facets that make Umbria an unparalleled destination.

Umbria's history is etched into the stones of its ancient towns. You've walked the same streets where Etruscans and Romans once roamed, admired frescoes that tell tales of faith and devotion, and stood in awe before architectural marvels that have weathered the ages. The spiritual aura of Assisi, the medieval grandeur of Gubbio, and the artistic vibrancy of Perugia have woven a tapestry of cultural heritage that's uniquely Umbrian.

Umbria's cuisine has tantalized your taste buds with its earthy flavors and regional specialties. You've savored truffle-infused delicacies, indulged in local olive oil, and relished hearty dishes that echo centuries-old traditions. From bustling markets to quaint trattorias, Umbria's culinary offerings have painted a vivid picture of the region's close relationship with its land and traditions.

Lake Trasimeno's serene waters and the lush countryside have offered moments of tranquility and outdoor exploration. The lively festivals, live music, and theatrical performances have added a vibrant note to your evenings, connecting you with the spirit of Umbria's people and their celebration of life.

From accommodation options that range from charming agriturismi to luxurious hotels, to transportation choices that span scenic train rides and convenient car rentals, you've navigated Umbria's landscapes with ease. You've familiarized yourself with currency, tipping etiquette, safety measures, and healthcare options, ensuring your comfort and well-being throughout your journey.

As you bid adieu to Umbria, remember that the experiences you've gathered here are not just souvenirs, but cherished stories that will weave themselves into the fabric of your own life's journey. Umbria's authenticity, its warm embrace, and its captivating beauty will remain with you, inspiring dreams of return and further exploration.

Buon viaggio! May your travels continue to be filled with wonder, discovery, and the joy of uncovering the world's hidden treasures. Until we meet again under the Italian sun, may the memories you've made in Umbria forever illuminate your path.

Printed in Great Britain
by Amazon

27907416R00079